In their nightly MENAGERIE À TROIS, DUFF, A RESCUED RACING GREYHOUND, AND BRUNO, A SMALLER ITALIAN GREYHOUND, GET COZY WITH BUSTER THE CAT, A BLACK-AND-WHITE SCOTTISH FOLD.

THE HUMANE SOCIETY OF NEW YORK WITH JULIA SZABO

PHOTOGRAPHS BY STANFORD T. WAN | FOREWORD BY ELISABETH RÖHM

WHERE ⋆Sleeping Dogs⋆ LIE

cozy CANINES and their NAPPING nests

stewart tabori & chang

NEW YORK

PROJECT EDITOR: SANDRA GILBERT
PRODUCTION DIRECTOR: KIM TYNER

PUBLISHED IN 2004 BY
STEWART, TABORI & CHANG
A COMPANY OF LA MARTINIÈRE GROUPE
115 WEST 18TH STREET
NEW YORK, NY 10011

CANADIAN DISTRIBUTION:
CANADIAN MANDA GROUP
ONE ATLANTIC AVENUE, SUITE 105
TORONTO, ONTARIO M67 3E7
CANADA

LIBRARY OF CONGRESS CATALOGING-IN-PUBLICATION DATA
SZABO, JULIA
WHERE SLEEPING DOGS LIE : COZY CANINES AND THEIR NAPPING NESTS / THE
HUMANE SOCIETY OF NEW YORK, WITH JULIA SZABO ; PHOTOGRAPHS BY STANFORD WAN;
FOREWORD BY ELISABETH RÖHM.
P. CM.
ISBN 1-58479-376-7 (HARDCOVER)
1. DOGS. 2. DOGS–BEHAVIOR. 3. BEDS. 4. DOGS–PICTORIAL WORKS.
I. WAN, STANFORD. II. HUMANE SOCIETY OF NEW YORK. III. TITLE.

SF416.S29 2004
636.7'0022'2–dc22
2004008996

DESIGN BY GOODESIGN
THE TEXT OF THIS BOOK WAS COMPOSED IN THE SANS AND LINOSCRIPT.

PRINTED IN CHINA

10 9 8 7 6 5 4 3 2 1
FIRST PRINTING

STEWART, TABORI & CHANG IS A SUBSIDIARY OF

Dedicated

★

TO ALL OF THE DOGS
(and cats) OF THE
HUMANE SOCIETY OF
NEW YORK

TWO OF THE SOCIETY'S ALUMNI ENJOYING THE BEST OF MANHATTAN: MIA THE FRENCH
BULLDOG GIVES TWO PAWS OF APPROVAL TO THE WESTIN TIMES SQUARE'S DOG
FRIENDLY ACCOMMODATIONS. SAMMY THE PEKINGESE SITS ON TOP OF THE WORLD AT
THE UPPER EAST SIDE PENTHOUSE THAT HE SHARES WITH CATHLEEN TOWERS SMITH.

As if the iconic Barcelona chair BY MIES VAN DER ROHE WEREN'T CHIC ENOUGH, SEAMUS THE SCOTTIE GETS EXTRA CUSHIONED SUPPORT FROM HIS WOOLLY PENDLETON BLANKET—A TARTAN IN HONOR OF HIS HERITAGE.

★ Contents ★

Water-mobile
for horses *(right)*,
circa 1905

Some beneficiaries of
a century of caring:
LEGENDARY ADOPTABLES, ARTHUR, GAWAIN,
AND MERLIN *(above)*

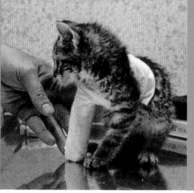

A tiny tabby kitten *(left)*,
her fractured foreleg
set in a cast, convalesces
at the Society's hospital.

Preface BY VIRGINIA CHIPURNOI

For more than one-hundred years, the Humane Society of New York has been a presence in New York City, caring for animals in need when illness, injury, or homelessness strikes. In 1904 we were founded to protect the city's horses against abuse. Members fought for laws to punish negligent owners and place watering troughs in streets and parks.

As funds allowed, the Society expanded to include a free medical clinic and a small adoption center for cats and dogs. Today our hospital and our Vladmir Horowitz and Wanda Toscanini Horowitz Adoption Center help more than 31,000 dogs and cats annually, and their numbers continue to grow.

On any given day the Humane Society of New York is responsible for hundreds of animals with diverse needs. For many, the Society is the only place where they will find help.

At the Society, the quality of each animal's life is paramount. Long before it was popular to think of animals as individuals—to consider their physical and emotional needs when taking responsibility for their care—*we* were doing just that. Today each dog has exercise time in the rooftop run and the chance to walk outdoors with staff and volunteers every day. Cats enjoy daily play sessions outside their kennels. This personal care is fully as important to a pet's well-being as the inoculations, spay/neuter, and other veterinary care provided during his or her stay in the adoption center. "This doesn't feel like a shelter," remark many visitors to the Society. "It feels like a home."

Julia Szabo understands all that animals bring to our lives. We thank her for caring, for being a good friend, and for producing such a charming book in support of the Society's work.

Animals are an important part of our social structure. They help define the place that we call home. Each day at the Humane Society of New York, we try to make life a little better for the animals that come to us for help. Our wish for all animals, everywhere, is a safe place to lay their heads at night.

President, The Humane Society of New York

Pillow Life BY ELISABETH RÖHM

My dog makes expressions that are so human, they even surpass the guilt of my own mother's caring eyes. Venus's amber-brown eyes, always with intent, work me into submission, the final result being a hug session in which her body is used as a pillow. The second we hit the ground or the bed, she inhales deeply and closes her eyes. It is then that I forgive her all the trespasses of puppydom. She sleeps. Shortly, I too will close my eyes, and our nap will commence. Although her sharklike jaw yawns directly in my face as we are nose-to-nose, I feel no fear. Being a Doberman is no easy task.

RÖHM WITH VENUS *(above)* AT THE W HOTEL TIMES SQUARE, NEW YORK CITY

This habit of reclining "where sleeping dogs lie" began when I was an infant. My mother had a white Boxer who was her baby before I hit the scene. As in *Lady and the Tramp*, Jenny made it her mission to be my great protector. She would baby-sit me while my parents meandered through some hippie-ish activity and were gone for hours. Jenny was always a part of my nap time. When I was old enough to climb out of my glamorous four-poster crib, my naps became our naps. I would lie down on the carpet—or the sand, or the grass—and nestle my head into her shoulder.

All these traditions I have passed on to Venus. At six weeks old, she became accustomed to the concept of pillow life. Before she was big enough to be my pillow, I was hers, and now, luckily for me, we trade. It is during these times that a long-overdue need for silence sets in. We rest.

I suggest if you are looking to bridge the gap between you and your dog, that you simply nap together. It's better than yoga for slowing down and collecting yourself. (It is also quite effective in human relationships. But then, everything I do well with people I learned from animals.)

Now, some of you may not have thought about this, but if you need to bridge a gap in yourself, I say get a dog! Forget what others might think about that not addressing your own loneliness. I believe getting a dog does address it. I ask you, who could say this type of relationship is unhealthy? From the beginning of time, mankind has turned to the dog species for companionship. It's in their soul to provide and to be needed by us.

And, what about dog shelters? Do you honestly think those dogs feel fulfilled, or that they have achieved their fullest doggie potential? I say not.

If you believe in empowerment of any kind, I suggest you adopt a shelter dog today. You will never know your or the dog's fullest potential until you do. Once you go home—and after you feed her, of course—lie down with your new friend and let her calm your nerves. The appreciation a dog must feel in accomplishing her natural duties is only surmounted by the reward you get in having a companion.

For all the friends I've had in between, I owe my love of animals to Jenny, who let me into the inner sanctum of "where sleeping dogs lie."

At the studio

OF ARTIST MARTHA SZABO, PEPPER DOES MODELING DUTY, RESTING HER HEAD
ON SAM. THE COUPLE RECLINE ON QUILTED MOVING BLANKETS, A COZY, INEXPENSIVE NEST
THAT DOGS CAN ARRANGE AND "CUSTOMIZE" ANY WHICH WAY THEY LIKE.

You Are Getting Sleepy BY JULIA SZABO

When I first met my dog Pepper, she was living on the street in the vicinity of East 86th Street and Third Avenue in Manhattan. I'd noticed her several times before—how daintily she lay on the sidewalk, curled up like a butter-caramel croissant, snoozing alongside a twentysomething homeless couple, her people. Then one day, on my way to the bank, I noticed a small crowd surrounding the croissant dog.

The homeless couple explained how circumstances forced them to get on a bus headed West, and they couldn't take their dog with them. If they didn't find someone to adopt her *that day*, Pepper (that was her name) would end up at the city pound, where the fate of owner-surrendered dogs was dismal at best. There were no takers, so I stepped forward. Never mind that I already had several dogs; I'm a sucker for a sweet pit bull. The young couple thanked me and went on their way; Pepper walked with me to the vet. She didn't look back.

As I got to know this remarkable dog, I learned how wonderfully easygoing she is, how affectionate, how generous with medicinal sloppy kisses and aerobic tail-wags. Her only quirk? She'd sooner die than eliminate on the sidewalk. In fact, the only place Pepper will "go" is as far from the curb as she can get—i.e., in the middle of the road, often perilously close to oncoming traffic.

This behavioral oddity puzzled me until I realized what it meant: Dogs never "go" where they sleep, and for as long as she could remember, Pepper's bed had been the sidewalk. It's been six years, and still Pepper steadfastly refuses to defile her old sleeping quarters.

Dogs are particular about where they sleep. Sure, they can get used to lying on cold, hard ground, but why should they? My dogs are not alone in gravitating to the coziest spots in the house. Like the rest of their species, they are experts in the field of creature comfort. These days, the Pepper-pot's favorite bed is anywhere my black dog, Sam, happens to be sleeping. Give these two some quilted moving blankets, and watch them cuddle up like the happy old marrieds they are.

The dogs you'll meet in this book all have their own intriguing bedtime stories. I am honored to be charged with the task of telling them.

A Gallery of Yawns

DOGS YAWN WHEN THEY ARE TIRED OR BORED, JUST LIKE WE DO. UNLIKE US, THEY DON'T FEEL COMPELLED TO COVER THEIR GAPING MAWS—AND WE LOVE THEM FOR IT.

These dogs lie in the lap OF LUXURY, YET THEY SEEM BLISSFULLY UNIMPRESSED BY IT ALL. MELVIN THE CHOCOLATE LAB (left) GETS READY TO CHASE A DREAM ON A BENCH COVERED IN FANCY DESIGNER LINEN FROM QUADRILLE. FANNY WAG THE MUTT (above) LOUNGES POOLSIDE IN THE HAMPTONS.

Carmen the Chihuahua, SUBJECT OF ARTIST JENNIFER WEINIK'S LIFE-SIZE CLASSICAL BRONZE STATUE *(background)*, WILL SOON GIVE IN TO SLEEP, APPEARING AS STILL AS THE LOVELY MONUMENT CREATED IN HER IMAGE.

Mr. Truman, the Bullmastiff, takes up more space THAN A WHOLE PACK OF SMALLER DOGS. STRETCHED LANGUIDLY ACROSS THE BED OF NEW YORK RESTAURATEURS PENNY AND PETER GLAZIER, HIS 132-POUND FRAME MAKES THE QUEEN-SIZE MATTRESS LOOK LIKE A LITTLE ARMY COT. WITH GIANT BREEDS, BE SURE YOUR BED IS BIG ENOUGH—AND THE MATTRESS STRONG ENOUGH—TO ACCOMMODATE ALL OF YOU.

Sweet Dreams

ON AVERAGE, DOGS SLEEP FROM TWELVE TO SIXTEEN HOURS DAILY. "THE PLACE A DOG RESTS HIS HEAD IS VERY IMPORTANT—IT'S THE CENTER OF HIS UNIVERSE," SAYS WILLIAM BERLONI, DIRECTOR OF ANIMAL BEHAVIOR AT THE HUMANE SOCIETY OF NEW YORK. "THE DENNING INSTINCT IS THE INSTINCT TO BE IN A PLACE WHERE YOU CAN CURL YOURSELF UP, CLOSE YOUR EYES, AND KNOW THAT YOU ARE TOTALLY SAFE FROM PREDATORS." THE BASIC REQUIREMENTS OF DOG OWNERSHIP ARE FOOD, WATER, SHELTER—AND A DOG BED.

"A dog needs that one spot where he can open his eyes to see the world in front of him, and close his eyes feeling his back is protected," Bill explains. "Sometimes dogs find that spot in the crook of your back on *your* bed, but all dogs want to have a space that they can call their own." Wherever that space is, whatever shape it takes, it's where your dog will display nesting behavior first displayed eons ago by his wolf ancestors: He'll circle a few times, maybe paw at the bed to fluff it up a bit, plop down, and shut his eyes. When that happens, your dog is telling you that all's well with the world; it's time for him to dream.

Swiss monks bred Saint Bernards
TO RESCUE STRANDED TRAVELERS ON SNOWY MOUNTAIN PASSES,
SO THEY'RE PERFECTLY IN THEIR ELEMENT OUTDOORS,
EVEN AT BEDTIME. IN FACT, SAINTS ARE QUITE UNCOMFORTABLE
IN HOT WEATHER AND MUST BE AIR-CONDITIONED OR THEY RUN THE RISK
OF SUFFERING HEAT STROKE. DEMONSTRATING HER BREED'S INNATE
AFFINITY FOR SNOW, BUOY LOVES TO LIE DOWN IN THE
SOFT WHITE STUFF, WITH A DUSTING OF FLAKES FROSTING HER BIG,
WIDE SNOUT. NOW, THERE'S A REAL SNOW ANGEL!

Sweet Dreams

Hugh the Australian Shepherd *(below)* demonstrates the denning instinct on a plush, cushioned Doggy Day Bed by For the Dogs.

For dogs who pant pitiably even in the dead of winter, there's an ingenious solution to beat the heat year-round: the Canine Cooler thermoregulating pet bed *(above)* . Simply fill it with water and it becomes a cool, cushioned nest for your hot dog.

For Lucy, a Shiba Inu,

IT'S ALL ABOUT ATMOSPHERE. HER FAVORITE PLACE

FOR A CATNAP IS THE BARE

WOOD FLOOR IN FRONT OF A ROARING FIRE.

Glamour Girls

HAVE ALWAYS LIVED BY A SIMPLE BEAUTY SECRET:
TO PROTECT YOUR HAIR AT BEDTIME, REST YOUR HEAD ON
NOTHING LESS THAN SATIN. THAT'S WHY SOPHIE,
A CHINESE CRESTED DOG, HAS A BED COVERED IN SILKY
RED SATIN, WHICH GUARDS HER TRESSES AGAINST BREAKAGE
AND STATIC. HERE, THE GORGEOUS PLATINUM
BLONDE STRIKES A POSE REMINISCENT OF YOUNG MARILYN
MONROE'S FAMOUS *PLAYBOY* PICTORIAL—JUST
CHECK OUT THOSE BEDROOM EYES.

Sophie

My brindle Pit Bull, Britannia Tige,

absolutely has to sleep on my bed, her head firmly planted on my pillow. She's grown accustomed to hogging the bed without shame. (Notice there's no quilt; that's because B enjoys gathering it up and pushing it to the floor.) Whenever she tires of my snoring, B retreats to the crawl space underneath the bed.

But I don't mind putting up with B's nocturnal antics. Two years ago, she was near death from a tetanus infection. After ten days in the animal hospital, she came home to complete her recovery, and ever since, the bed has been her sanctum sanctorum. For as long as she needs it, my bed will be hers too.

During B's recovery, I slept with one eye open, monitoring my dog for possible seizures. Pretty soon, I forgot what it was like to rest, and all that sleep deprivation took its toll on my other dogs and me. Luckily, we discovered Susan Raimond.

The California harpist has recorded five soothing CDs of harp music she's compiled to calm anxious animals at shelters, hospitals, and zoos. From dogs and cats to birds and giraffes, all have succumbed to slumber in minutes. This is not just music: "It's a tool for stress reduction and pain management," Susan explains. "Whatever you do, don't play this music while driving!" Now all we need to do is put on *Wait for the Sunset* and B and I are out like two lights. It's the most important CD in my collection; whenever my animals seem stressed, I put it on and within about thirteen minutes, our kingdom is peaceable once more.

On the other hand, Nero,

AN AMERICAN BULLDOG *(below)*, LOVES TO FEEL
SNUGLY TUCKED IN, SO HE SURROUNDS
HIMSELF WITH SWEET SHEETS THE COLOR OF
STRAWBERRY ICE CREAM.

Britannia Tige

HATES TO FEEL CONFINED *(above)*. SHE PREFERS
A TRADITIONAL FLORAL BED WITH
MINIMAL TO NO BED CLOTHES—AND A NICE,
FLUFFY PILLOW OR TWO.

Doesn't everyone dream of sleeping

WITH A MODEL? FOR THIS QUARTET OF LUCKY DOGS, THAT FANTASY IS A NIGHTLY
REALITY. "I CAN'T SLEEP WITHOUT MY BABIES," SAYS KRISTINE SZABO,
WHO SHARES HER BED WITH RAT TERRIERS MADELINE, MOBY, STUMPY, AND SWEEDY.
"WHEN I STAY IN A HOTEL ALONE," SHE ADDS, "I HAVE TO SURROUND MYSELF
WITH PILLOWS, BECAUSE I NEED SOMETHING TO HOLD ON TO!"

Sleeping Together

MANY DOG LOVERS WOULDN'T DREAM OF SLEEPING WITHOUT AT LEAST ONE FOUR-LEGGED BEDMATE. AFTER A HARD DAY, THERE'S NOTHING SO CALMING AS THE SOUND OF A GENTLY SNORING HOUND. DOGS' NORMAL BODY TEMPERATURE RANGES BETWEEN 100 AND 102 DEGREES FAHRENHEIT, WHILE FOR HUMANS IT'S A MERE 98.6—SO IN WINTER, OUR DOGS DOUBLE AS HIGHLY EFFICIENT BED-WARMERS. PLUS, IT'S GREAT FUN TO SPOON WITH THEM. WHAT'S IN IT FOR THE PETS? PLENTY. "DOGS LIKE SLEEPING CLOSE TO THE PACK LEADER," SAYS WILLIAM BERLONI. "A WOLF ALLOWS THE CLOSEST MEMBERS OF HIS PACK TO SLEEP NEAR HIM FOR SAFETY AND WARMTH, AND DOGS SLEEPING WITH THEIR HUMANS REPLICATE THAT. FOR DOGS TO SHARE OUR BEDS BRINGS THEM CLOSER TO US AS COMPANIONS."

It's not easy getting some dogs into bed. They're not playing hard to get. They need a leg up, especially if they are elderly. Breeds with long bodies and short legs, such as dachshunds and basset hounds, need extra help getting down from the bed, because they run the risk of injuring their spines by jumping. Whether Fido is getting on or off the bed, help him reach his goal safely.

On the decorating front, there are a few key points to remember when making a bed paw-friendly. First, protect the mattress with a zip-up mattress protector and at least one mattress pad (my dogs' favorite is one made of organic wool from a company called Lifekind—so far, nothing's penetrated it). Keep at least two sets of sheets and two extra duvet covers, in case an "accident" necessitates a quick change. High-thread-count bed linens are well worth their higher price tag. They're tightly woven, so pet hairs stay on the surface for easy removal. Consider floral bedding, as the patterns are very forgiving of accident stains. (My dogs prefer the vibrant colors of sheets by Kim Parker Home.) Finally, the best bedspread is one made of matelasse; the dense quilting is attractive, elegant, and durable enough to stand up to heavy pawing and clawing.

Right

Wrong

Bill Berloni has some valuable advice for couples:

"The one thing you don't want is any dog sleeping between you; that tells the dog he's controlling the relationship. Have your dog sleep at the foot of the bed or off to one side, never in between you and your partner."

If you're single and dating, it's a good idea to close the dog out of the bedroom once every two weeks. Though it may break your heart at first, this routine can go a long way toward introducing your pet into a new relationship. "If you have an overnight guest and you close the door on your pet occasionally, it won't be as much of a shock—and the pet won't resent the new person," Bill explains. Some dogs, he adds, "get very agitated when their owner is being 'mounted.'"

CASSIDY THE MUTT AND HER HUMANS, ELANA FRANKEL AND DAN TASHMAN, DEMONSTRATE THE BEHAVIORALLY CORRECT AND INCORRECT WAY FOR COUPLES TO SLEEP WITH A DOG.

Some dog beds make cozy napping nests

FOR PEOPLE TOO. THIS CIRCULAR GREEN BED IS

BIG ENOUGH FOR SIMKA THE BORZOI TO SHARE WITH HER FAVORITE

FOUR-YEAR-OLD, ROWAN CAMPBELL SMART.

For kids who are afraid of the dark, A SLEEPING DOG IS THE MOST DEPENDABLE SECURITY BLANKET. SIX-YEAR-OLD JENNA BERLONI SLEEPS WITH A BASENJI NAMED SADIE. AS JENNA LIKES TO TELL HER FRIENDS, "MY DOG KEEPS THE MONSTERS AWAY." TALK ABOUT A TRUSTY WATCHDOG!

Sleeping Together

Dogs help give confidence to children. Even asleep, Emily the Golden Retriever *(below)* makes young Max Halpern feel so self-assured, he looks like a mogul-in-the-making, chatting away on Mommy's cell phone.

My old hound mix, Hound *(above)*, isn't getting any younger. His tired, aching joints appreciate the Scamp Ramp, which enables him to reach the bed and sofa with greater ease (plus, it comes in a range of stylish covers like this white-and-black toile).

Sleeping with the enemy?

SHHH... DON'T TELL THAT TO MADDIE THE DOG AND
PUSHKIN THE CAT, WHO ADORE EACH OTHER.
IN FACT, BACK WHEN SHE USED TO BE THE ONLY PET,
MADDIE SUFFERED FROM SEVERE SEPARATION ANXIETY.
THEN HER FAMILY ADOPTED PUSHKIN. AND EVER
SINCE PUSHKIN CAME HOME, MADDIE'S BEEN SO HAPPY
TO HAVE A FULL-TIME PLAYMATE—AND
BEDMATE!—THAT ALL HER TROUBLESOME ISSUES
ARE NOW RESOLVED.

Seamus the Wheaten Scottie

SEES EYE-TO-EYE—MAKE THAT TAIL-TO-TAIL—WITH A GINGHAM

SCOTTIE TOY BY HARRY BARKER.

Sometimes a cold, hard, inanimate object

MAKES A FINE SLEEPING COMPANION, AS SKY THE WIRE-HAIRED FOX TERRIER

PROVES BY SNOOZING WITH A STONE CAT.

Sleeping surrounded by
ONE'S FAVORITE THINGS IS ALWAYS COMFORTING.
SOME DOGS HAVEN'T GOT ENOUGH TOYS;
CLEARLY, THAT IS NOT FIFI THE MINIATURE PINSCHER'S PROBLEM!

With one paw resting on a Fu-dog finial
AND A JADE PENDANT HANGING FROM HIS COLLAR,
XIAO LONG HAS THE AIR OF A FOUR-LEGGED EMPEROR.

Sleeping in Style

MARIE ANTOINETTE'S TINY PAPILLON SLEPT IN A SPLENDID, VELVET-COVERED "KENNEL" THAT NOW RE-
SIDES IN THE METROPOLITAN MUSEUM OF ART IN MANHATTAN. TODAY'S PAMPERED PETS HAVE
EQUALLY REGAL DIGS. THE MORE FASHION-CONSCIOUS THE DOG LOVER, THE MORE STYLISH HER DOG'S
BED WILL BE. IN FACT, MANY CHIC INTERIORS BOAST DOG BEDS THAT ARE EVERY BIT AS LAVISH AS THE
MOST EXPENSIVE DESIGNER FURNISHINGS FOR HUMANS. A DOG'S BED HAS BECOME AN EXPRESSION OF
HIS HUMAN'S PERSONALITY, TASTE, AND STYLE. BUT MOST IMPORTANT, WE SHOW HOW MUCH WE
LOVE OUR DOGS BY HOW MUCH TIME, EFFORT, AND YES, MONEY WE LAVISH ON THEIR BEDDING.
NO MATTER WHAT THE COST, FOR A DOG TO HAVE HIS OWN SLEEPING PLACE IS PRICELESS. AS BILL
BERLONI EXPLAINS, "IT'S THE PLACE WHERE HE FEELS WARM AND SECURE."

Centuries ago, the diminutive Japanese Chin kept company with the ladies of the imperial
Chinese court. One of the Chinese emperors had given a Chin as a gift to the emperor of Japan,
which is how the breed got its name. Today, these delightful dogs warm the laps—and hearts—of
people from all walks of life all over the world. Inspired by the noble heritage of her Chin, Xiao
Long (Mandarin for "Little Dragon"), Laura Lobdell created this chinoiserie niche *(opposite)*, lovingly
upholstering and hand-painting it inside and out, front and back. Some dogs respond to the
command "lie down;" others hit the sack when they're told "go to bed" or "beddy-bye." But Laura
merely says "château," and Xiao Long knows exactly where to go. His bed really is his castle.

A real label hound, CARMEN THE CHIHUAHUA LOUNGES ON AN OTTOMAN BY HARRY BERTOIA *(left)*; BEHIND HER IS THE MATCHING BERTOIA BIRD HIGH-BACK CHAIR, A DESIGN ICON SINCE 1952; IT'S DRAPED WITH AN ERTÉ-INSPIRED SILK SCARF THAT'S VINTAGE EMILIO PUCCI.

Carmen is also welcome ON THE BED *(above)*, OUTFITTED WITH ANTIQUE DAMASK LINENS AND EMBROIDERED PILLOWCASES. BUT WHEN SHE'S SERIOUS ABOUT SLUMBER ON A DOG-DAY AFTERNOON, CARMEN CATCHES HER Z'S ON A MINIATURE WROUGHT-IRON BED *(left)* DRESSED IN LUXE LINEN AND SILK.

Sleeping In Style

Three dog night: Nancy Tsuei was so inspired by the nesting instincts of her little Malteses *(above)* that she designed a collection of colorful dog beds, Pie Pie Pillows, just for miniature breeds. Betty, Pumbaa, and JJ certainly appreciate her efforts.

A clean, dust-free bedroom is the most stylish place to sleep. Sweep clean with the Dyson DC07 Animal *(below)*, designed specifically for people with pets.

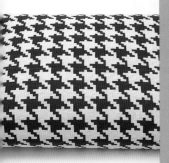

Who says Shih Tzus can't rough it? Mica and Jynx settle down on this military-inspired travel blanket by The Life of Ryley *(below)* that's anything but standard-issue (check out the cushy fleece backing).

The outdoorsy type, Tonto the Shiba Inu *(below)* is happy to "camp out" in her very own indoor teepee.

What could be more fitting for a hound than a dapper custom cushion made of houndstooth fabric by Diamond & Barratta Design *(above)*?

Designer Tara Boone's handbags are favorites of Jennifer Garner, Molly Sims, and Heidi Klum—and Tara's two beloved Shih Tzus, Roscoe and Duncan *(above)*. Here, the dogs take "sleeping in style" quite literally, curling right up in a glamorous tote bag that Tara casually left on a chair.

Sometimes, the most stylish fabrics
ARE ALSO, SURPRISINGLY, THE MOST DURABLE.
CASSIUS THE RHODESIAN RIDGEBACK RELAXES ON A CHAISE
COVERED IN SUMPTUOUS COBALT MOHAIR VELVET.

Mr. Truman the Bullmastiff
COUCH POTATO PREFERS HIS

MOHAIR IN VIBRANT EMERALD GREEN.

Fanny Wag is a Hamptons celebrity,
A RESCUED MUTT WITH HER VERY OWN VEGETARIAN
DOG BISCUIT NAMED AFTER HER.
AS BEFITS A FOUR-LEGGED STAR, FANNY WAG CAN LUXURIATE
ALFRESCO ON HER CHOICE OF CUSHIONED SETTEE.

⋆Fanny Wag⋆

Lounging poolside at home
IN EAST HAMPTON, BAILEY THE MUTT LOOKS READY FOR HIS
CLOSE-UP IN *TOWN & COUNTRY*. BUT WHEN THE SUN IS HIGH,
HE WISELY TAKES COVER *UNDER* THE TEAK DECK CHAIR.

She can sleep on a pillow
MADE OF GOLDEN CORD
CREATED BY THE ARTIST CHUCK PRICE.

Ann the Jack Russell Terrier
CAN SLEEP ANYWHERE SHE LIKES—ON A
LAVENDER NAUGAHYDE DAYBED, FOR EXAMPLE.

Plus, she enjoys playing
PRINCESS-AND-THE-PEA ON A STACK OF TARGET CORDUROY CUSHIONS
BY HER ALL-TIME FAVORITE DESIGNER *(and doting dad)*, TODD OLDHAM.

Where's Snowball? The Dalmatian mix *(below)* virtually disappears on a swank custom bed made of "Geometri" fabric, created in 1960 by the Danish design legend Verner Panton. Just call this designer dog the Panton Dalmatian!

When selecting a place for your dog to lie, it's fun to play with ethnic affinity. Why not give your Brittany spaniels a dog bed covered in Provençal toile de Jouy *(below)*? Très Français!

Fashion hounds simply must keep up appearances while on the go. Isaac the Yorkie *(above)* does the town in a Petote bag.

This red toile and gingham dog bed, with coordinating toile Dachshund toy *(above)*, is by Harry Barker.

Chinese breeds, including Chow Chows, Shar-Peis, and Chinese Cresteds, will feel right at home on the Asian-style Zen bed by Scout & Hunter *(below)*, accessorized with Bodhi's bamboo-shaped chew toys and "carved" rubber balls.

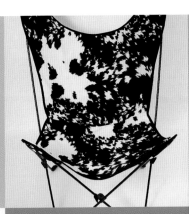

One is never too young for a stylish bed. English Bulldog pup Maggie *(below)* fits snugly in a Moses basket made especially for dog babies, complete with a cuddly chenille receiving blanket.

The butterfly chair *(above)* has been a design icon since 1938, but it's not the most comfortable place for people to park. Small dogs, on the other hand, love this chair. It feels like a cozy hammock, as Maggie the Lhasa Apso proves.

Design-conscious dog lovers can get creative by covering the butterfly frame in a wide range of fabrics, including off-the-rack (Marimekko for Crate & Barrel) or custom Ultrasuede *(above)*.

These days, Headley the star Pit Bull
DOESN'T SEEK OUT THE LIMELIGHT; HE'S HAPPY TO
HANG OUT UNDER HIS PIZZA OVEN AND SNACK ON RAW CARROTS.

Sleeping Around

DOGS OFTEN CONK OUT IN THE MOST UNEXPECTED PLACES. CONSIDER THIS PIT BULL, HAPPILY SLEEPING UNDER A PIZZA OVEN AT HIS OWNER'S RESTAURANT, CJ'S PIZZA, IN KILLINGWORTH, CONNECTICUT. ABANDONED IN BROOKLYN FOUR YEARS AGO, THE DOG WAS FOUND WANDERING THROUGH PROSPECT PARK AND BROUGHT TO THE HUMANE SOCIETY OF NEW YORK. SHORTLY AFTER HIS ARRIVAL, HE CROSSED PATHS WITH WILLIAM BERLONI, AND A STAR WAS BORN. BILL KNOWS CANINE TALENT WHEN HE SEES IT; HE'S FAMOUS FOR HAVING DISCOVERED A CERTAIN MUTT NAMED SANDY, THE FOUR-LEGGED STAR OF BROADWAY'S *ANNIE*. BILL NAMED THE PIT BULL HEADLEY BECAUSE, WELL, BECAUSE HIS HEAD WAS NOT SMALL. LITTLE DID HEADLEY KNOW HIS HEAD WOULD SOON HAVE THE OPPORTUNITY TO GROW EVEN BIGGER!

Just one week after Bill discovered Headley, the noted theater director Martha Clarke was planning to adapt the 1952 movie *Hans Christian Andersen* for the stage and asked Bill to find her a large dog that, in the Andersen character's words, has "eyes as big as pinwheels." Headley was the fourth dog Clarke auditioned—and he got the part on the spot.

"When the show's producers met Headley, they said, 'You adopted him from an animal shelter a week ago?!'" Bill recalls. "I find pit bulls to be the easiest dog to train of any breed I've worked with, both in terms of intelligence and devotion. And true to his breed, Headley is a brilliant dog.'"

Nothing says summer LIKE A NAP ON THE BEACH. IN WAINSCOTT, NEW YORK, SKY THE WIRE-HAIRED FOX TERRIER SUNBATHES ON HER FAVORITE BEACH TOWEL. PLEASE PASS THE SUNSCREEN! *(Sky's favorite brand is Fauna SPF 15 with tea tree and lavender oil, for pets and people to share.)*

★Sky★

Salty Paws II

East Hampton, NY

CARVER

Vicky Winslow *(below)* strides along the busy streets of Manhattan, navigates the complicated subway system with ease, and stops to take the occasional coffee break at an outdoor cafe. She's no different from most busy New Yorkers, except she's been blind since birth. By her side at all times is her beloved guide, a German Shepherd named Gina. "I don't just love her for the work she does," Vicky says. "She's simply one of the best dogs I've ever had." Don't let that "sleeping dog" pose fool you. With her sensitive ears and nose, Gina is alert and vigilant. Even with her eyes closed, she's looking out for Vicky.

Moored in Sag Harbor,

THE SALTY PAWS II (left) IS NAMED FOR TAFFY THE COCKER SPANIEL *(above)*, WHO FREQUENTLY NAPS ON THE BRIDGE. SHE'S A FIRST-RATE FIRST MATE!

Theodora, a.k.a. Teddy, is a Dalmatian
WHO LOST HER RIGHT FORELEG TO CANCER IN 1999. NOW THAT SHE'S TEN, ARTHRITIS MAKES
WALKING DIFFICULT AND PAINFUL, SO LONG WALKS ARE NOT AN OPTION.
INSTEAD, TEDDY LETS OTHERS DO THE WALKING, TAKING IT EASY IN A RADIO FLYER WAGON EQUIPPED
WITH A CUSTOM PADDED CUSHION TO EASE HER SWOLLEN JOINTS, PLUS A
HANDY BOTTLE OF DRINKING WATER AND A SUPPLY OF TEDDY'S DOG TREATS, THE POPULAR
PUPPY BISCUITS CREATED TO PLEASE HER DISCERNING PALATE.

For longer trips, Teddy travels by car;
HERE SHE LOOKS ABOUT READY TO SLEEP AT THE WHEEL OF HER NEIGHBOR'S 1966 DODGE
CORONET. A TRUE FASHION HOUND CAN'T GO OUT WITHOUT COORDINATING
ACCESSORIES, SO YOU'LL NOTICE, DANGLING FROM THE REARVIEW MIRROR, A PAIR
OF FUZZY DICE TO MATCH TEDDY'S DOTTY BLACK-AND-WHITE COAT.

Freshly mown grass makes
A SWEET-SMELLING BED, AS BAILEY THE
MUTT DEMONSTRATES. JUST BE SURE TO EXAMINE
DOGS FOR TICKS AFTER THEY'VE BEEN LYING
DOWN OUTDOORS, ESPECIALLY DURING TICK SEASON,
WHICH LASTS FROM MAY THROUGH OCTOBER.
KEEP A BOTTLE OF VODKA IN THE FREEZER; IF YOUR DOG
HAS A TICK, SPLASH ICE-COLD VODKA ON THE
AREA TO IMMOBILIZE THE VARMINT.
THEN REMOVE THE TICK WITH TWEEZERS.

Sleeping Around

At Noonan Antiques in Hudson, New York, Walter the mutt *(below)* wears a silk cravat and gets some shuteye on a nineteenth-century invalid's chair.

Traveling by car can be so tiresome. That's why Mindy the English Springer Spaniel *(above)* leaves the driving to someone else. She prefers to sleep through the trip in the back of her Volvo station wagon.

...then he takes a swing
IN THE HAMMOCK *(below)*...FINALLY, HE OPTS
FOR A MORE CUSHIONED, STATIONARY NEST:
THE DECK CHAIR *(opposite page)*.

On a hot summer day,
RALPH THE BOXER MOVES RESTLESSLY IN SEARCH
OF THE PERFECT SLEEPING SPOT. FIRST HE COOLS
OFF ON A STONE TILE IN THE GARDEN *(above)*.

Rufus, a Münsterlander pup,
IS AN EXTRAORDINARILY HEAVY SLEEPER.
HE CAN FALL ASLEEP ANYWHERE: IN LINE AT THE BANK,
ON THE KITCHEN FLOOR, OR IN THE BATHROOM,
WHERE THE ONYX TILE IS NICE AND COOL
AND THERE'S ALWAYS SOMEONE TO WASH OVER HIM.

In the wake of September 11, 2001,

the staff and volunteers of the Humane Society of New York were on the scene at Ground Zero, witnessing first-hand how courageous New Yorkers came together to help rescue companion animals trapped in crumbling buildings. But heroes don't just walk on two legs; many of the bravest volunteers during those terrible days were hard-working canines. Whether trained for search and rescue or for therapy work, these dogs inspired us with their dedication and heart, searching through the rubble and bringing comfort to those who had lost family and friends.

Courageous working dogs
DON'T LIE DOWN ON THE JOB—BUT EVEN
THEY NEED TO TAKE A WELL-DESERVED BREAK
ONCE IN A WHILE.

Tikva the Keeshond *(below)*,
a therapy dog

Oz *(right)*, a drug-sniffing
dog with U.S. Customs
d Border Protection, puts the
"American" in American
it Bull Terrier. (He was not at
Ground Zero, but he is no
less a courageous canine.)
Here, Oz gets horizontal
in the shade.

Search and Rescue
dogs Phantom, a Border Collie,
and Taz, a black Lab *(above)*

Cody the Great Pyrenees
IS THE DRAW AT PARK AVENUE'S PLAZA FLORIST
WHERE SCHOOL CHILDREN STOP
BY TO SAY HELLO TO "THE FLOWER DOG."

The Desk Set

EVERY YEAR IN JUNE, MANY OFFICES TAKE PART IN "TAKE YOUR DOG TO WORK DAY" TO ENCOURAGE PETLESS CO-WORKERS TO ADOPT SHELTER DOGS. BUT SOME DOGS WE KNOW GO TO THE OFFICE EVERY DAY OF THE YEAR. AND YES, THEY ALL LIE DOWN ON THE JOB—BUT THAT DOESN'T MEAN THEY'RE NOT PRODUCTIVE.

At the headquarters of decorative hardware specialist E. R. Butler, a regal Doberman named Lena *(right)* isn't afraid to be caught yawning during office hours (she's the boss's pet and she knows it). At the PR firm Krupp Kommunications, Isaac the Yorkie *(above)* makes a handsome desk accessory.

Scarlet, a Boston-based Jack Russell Terrier,
IS A FREQUENT FLYER WHO'S TRAVELED THE WORLD—BUT OTHER
THAN HOME, HER FAVORITE PLACE TO SPEND THE NIGHT IS THE W HOTEL TIMES SQUARE.

Do Not Disturb

THE STARWOOD HOTEL GROUP DOESN'T JUST WELCOME DOGS; THE HOSPITALITY GIANT ROLLS OUT THE RED CARPET FOR FOUR-LEGGED TRAVELERS. STARWOOD'S PROPERTIES—INCLUDING THE W, WESTIN, AND SHERATON—ALL PROVIDE SPECIAL BOWLS FOR FOOD AND WATER, PLUS DESIGNER DOG BEDS BY ELOISE, THE CALIFORNIA COMPANY WHOSE SATISFIED CUSTOMERS INCLUDE THE PETS OF DARYL HANNAH AND DEBRA MESSING. IN AN UNPRECEDENTED DECORATING FLOURISH, THE HOTEL DOG BEDS COORDINATE WITH THE ROOMS' STYLISH INTERIORS.

Once your dog is sleeping soundly, especially in such "heavenly" surroundings, let her dream on and on. And, always remember not to rouse your pup too abruptly from her slumber—sometimes, it really is best to let sleeping dogs lie.

Stage, Screen, and TV actor

SAM WATERSTON, A STAR OF *LAW AND ORDER*, ENJOYS GETTING TO KNOW KENYA,
A MELLOW SENIOR DOG, UP FOR ADOPTION FROM THE SOCIETY.

Many dog-loving New Yorkers

GO DOGLESS BECAUSE THEY FEAR THEIR BUSY SCHEDULES WON'T LEAVE THEM TIME FOR
A DOG. NOT ELISABETH RÖHM OF TV'S *LAW AND ORDER*. HER OFF-SET TIME IS SPENT
WITH HER BEST FRIEND: A DOBERMAN NAMED VENUS. THAT INCLUDES HUGGING, KISSING,
AND NUZZLING IN BED TOGETHER AT THE W HOTEL. "I BRING HER EVERYWHERE,"
ELISABETH EXPLAINS. "IN NEW YORK YOU DON'T HAVE TO LEAVE DOGS AT HOME."

Jackie, a dog up for adoption
AT THE HUMANE SOCIETY OF NEW YORK, GETS COMFORTABLE
WITH *LAW AND ORDER* STAR JESSE MARTIN
ON THE ELEGANT "RÊVE" CANOPY BED AT CATHERINE MEMMI'S
ULTRA-CHIC LIFESTYLE STORE IN MANHATTAN'S SOHO.
NOW THAT'S THE STUFF OF SWEET DREAMS.

KRISTINE SZABO RECEIVES NIGHTLY FACIALS FROM HER *sleepy pack of terriers.*

Good-Night Kisses

It's true that dogs often put their tongues in unmentionable places. Licking is their way of checking things out. But dogs also express love by licking other dogs and people, just as humans express love with kisses. "Dogs lick for parental reasons," explains William Berloni. "It's nurturing—whether it's to clean us, cool us, calm us, or greet us—and it's what parent dogs do to their pups and other creatures they care for. We should be honored that they consider us worthy of such an intimate gesture." So don't resist your dog's kisses; such displays of affection are good for both of you. Interestingly, dogs are less likely than our fellow humans to pass on infections; they have fewer germs in their mouths than people do. Some dogs can, however, carry bacteria and parasites that might make a person sick (especially a person with a compromised immune system), so it's not a good idea to kiss a strange dog full on the mouth with your lips open. But a loving kiss from your own healthy, happy dog—whose teeth are, hopefully, brushed with some regularity!—is the sweetest kiss of all.

Good Night Kisses

Basset Hounds
Ben and Emma *(right)*
wax romantic
prior to nodding off.

Whether you walk on four
legs or two, there's nothing quite
as luxurious as a custom bed.
Pugs Mona and Nina share
one covered in "Pugs and Petals"
linen, a deluxe fabric created in
their honor by the textile firm
Lee Jofa *(above and right)*.
The Pug pals lick each other before
settling in for the night.

Resource Guide

MILITARY-INSPIRED TRAVEL BLANKET BY THE LIFE OF RYLEY, AVAILABLE FROM FETCH, 43 GREENWICH AVENUE, NEW YORK CITY, (212) 352-8591, OR GO TO WWW.THELIFEOFRYLEY.COM

FOR STORES CARRYING TARA BOONE HANDBAGS, GO TO WWW.TARABOONE.COM

TEEPEE BY WAGWEAR AVAILABLE AT FETCH, 43 GREENWICH AVENUE, NEW YORK CITY, (212) 352-8591, OR GO TO WWW.FETCHPETS.COM

PAGE 46
FANNY WAG BISCUITS AVAILABLE FROM SYLVESTER & COMPANY, 103 MAIN STREET, SAG HARBOR, NEW YORK, (631) 725-5012

PAGE 52
PETOTE AVAILABLE AT FETCH, 32 GREENWICH AVENUE, NEW YORK CITY, (212) 352-8591, OR GO TO WWW.PETOTE.COM

DOG BED MADE BY CAMILLE CASARETTI INC., (718) 875-3111, OF "GEOMETRI" FABRIC BY VERNER PANTON, AVAILABLE TO THE TRADE FROM MAHARAM, (800) 645-3943, OR GO TO WWW.MAHARAM.COM

TOILE AND GINGHAM DOG BED AND COORDINATING TOILE DACHSHUND TOY BY HARRY BARKER, (800) HI-HARRY, WWW.HARRYBARKER.COM

PAGE 53
BUTTERFLY CHAIR WITH SPOTTED ORANGE MARIMEKKO COVER AVAILABLE AT CRATE & BARREL, WWW.CRATEANDBARREL.COM

"COWHIDE" PATTERN COVER CUSTOM MADE BY CAMILLE CASARETTI INC., (718) 875-3111, OF ULTRASUEDE, OR GO TO WWW.ULTRASUEDE.COM

ZEN BED BY SCOUT & HUNTER AND BODHI TOYS FROM FETCH, 43 GREENWICH AVENUE, NEW YORK CITY (212) 352-8591, OR GO TO WWW.FETCHPETS.COM

MOSES BASKET AND CHENILLE RECEIVING BLANKET FROM WWW.SCAMPSONLINE.COM

Chapter 4: Sleeping Around

PAGE 57
FAUNA GROOMING PRODUCTS, (800) 536-1909, OR GO TO WWW.FAUNAPET.COM

PAGE 60
RADIO FLYER WAGON AVAILABLE AT TOYS R US STORES, WWW.TOYSRUS.COM, OR GO TO WWW.RADIOFLYER.COM

RED CUSHION CUSTOM-MADE BY CAMILLE CASARETTI INC., (718) 875-3111

TEDDY'S DOG TREATS AVAILABLE AT WWW.TEDDYSDOGTREATS.COM

PAGE 63
MIDNIGHT-BLUE DENIM DOG BED WITH "SLEEPING AROUND" MONOGRAM BY CAMILLE CASARETTI INC., (718) 875-3111

Chapter 5: Do Not Disturb

PAGE 72
TO CONTACT STARWOOD HOTELS, VISIT WWW.STARWOOD.COM

DOG BEDS BY ELOISE AT FETCH, 43 GREENWICH AVENUE, NEW YORK CITY, (212) 352-8591, OR GO TO WWW.ELOISEINC.COM

PAGE 77
RÊVE CANOPY BED FROM CATHERINE MEMMI, 45 GREENE STREET, NEW YORK CITY, (212) 226-8200, OR GO TO WWW.CATHERINEMEMMI.COM

PAGE 78
PAINTING (ABOVE BED), "CANINE QUARTET" BY MARTHA SZABO, WWW.MARTHASZABO.COM

PAGE 80
MIDNIGHT-BLUE DENIM DOG BED WITH "GOOD NIGHT KISSES" MONOGRAM BY CAMILLE CASARETTI INC., (718) 875-3111

"PUGS AND PETALS" FABRIC AVAILABLE TO THE TRADE FROM LEE JOFA, WWW.LEEJOFA.COM

PAGE 82 (top row, left to right)
DOG BED BY BURBERRY, (877) 832-6300, OR GO TO WWW.BURBERRY.COM

SNUGGALUVS BED FROM FETCH, 43 GREENWICH AVENUE, NEW YORK CITY, (212) 352-8591, OR GO TO WWW.SNUGGALUVS.COM

GINGHAM DOG BED WITH COORDINATING TOILE DACHSHUND TOY FROM HARRY BARKER, (800) HI-HARRY, OR GO TO WWW.HARRYBARKER.COM

(middle row, left to right): ORANGE PLASTIC BREAD TRAY FROM T. M. FITZGERALD CO., (888) 795-0660, OR GO TO WWW.TMFITZGERALD.COM (SHOWN WITH BLUE QUILTED MOVING BLANKET FROM MOVERS SUPPLY HOUSE INC., 800-432-1MSH)

BUTTERFLY DOG BED FROM JONATHAN ADLER, WWW.JONATHANADLER.COM

TARTAN DOG BED FROM ORVIS, (888) 235-9763, OR GO TO WWW.ORVIS.COM

(bottom row, left to right): GOOD DOG BED FROM GEORGE, SAN FRANCISCO, (877) 322-3232, OR GO TO WWW.GEORGESF.COM

DOGGY DAY BED BY FOR THE DOGS FROM FETCH, 43 GREENWICH AVENUE, NEW YORK CITY, (212) 352-8591, OR GO TO WWW.FETCHPETS.COM

ORANGE BETTIE DOG TOYS AND SNUGGALUVS BED FROM FROM FETCH, 43 GREENWICH AVENUE, NEW YORK CITY, (212) 352-8591

PAGE 85
BURROWING DOG BED BY GASTON AVAILABLE AT TRIXIE + PEANUT PET EMPORIUM, 23 EAST 20TH STREET, NEW YORK CITY, (212) 358-0881, OR GO TO WWW.TRIXIEANDPEANUT.COM

PAGE 88
MIDNIGHT-BLUE DENIM DOG BED WITH "DO NOT DISTURB" MONOGRAM BY CAMILLE CASARETTI INC., (718) 875-3111

Back Cover

(top left):
SNUGGALUVS BED AND LOTUS TOYS BY BODHI, AVAILABLE FROM FETCH, 43 GREENWICH AVENUE, NEW YORK CITY, (212) 352-8591, OR GO TO WWW.FETCHPETS.COM

(bottom right):
MIDNIGHT-BLUE DENIM DOG BED WITH "NIGHTY-NIGHT" MONOGRAM BY CAMILLE CASARETTI INC., (718) 875-3111

Jacket Flap

COTTAGE GARDEN BED BY PAMELA SCURRY FROM VAUGHAN FURNITURE CO., (276) 236-6111 or WWW.VAUGHANFURNITURE.COM

Dachshunds really know how to

TUCK THEMSELVES IN FOR THE NIGHT. TENACIOUS LITTLE "WIENERDOGS" WERE
BRED TO HUNT BADGERS, FOLLOWING THEIR QUARRY DOWN LONG, UNDER-
GROUND HOLES AND FIGHTING TO THE DEATH, IF NECESSARY. NO WONDER DOXIES
LOVE BURROWING DEEP UNDER THE BEDCLOTHES—THEY'RE
HARD-WIRED TO DO SO! NEW YORK DESIGNER GASTON, A BIG FAN OF THE BREED,
CREATED THE BURROWING DOG BED, AN HAUTE SLEEPING BAG FOR SMALL DOGS.
IT'S MODELED HERE BY GASTON'S FOXY DOXIE, ALLORA.

Rat Terrier Moby
IS BARELY VISIBLE IN A SEA OF STONE-GRAY
CALVIN KLEIN BEDDING.

Acknowledgments

We're grateful to all the people who generously donated their dogs' time for these photographs. Special thanks for the divine interventions of Yvonna Balfour and Nora Elcar. Woofs to Leslie Stoker and Sandy Gilbert of Stewart, Tabori & Chang, Kathryn Hammill and Diane Shaw of Goodesign, Elisabeth Röhm, Marcy Engelman, Marissa Mastellone, Starwood Hotel Group, Andrea Fairweather/Fairweather Faces, Carole Wilbourn, and the tireless people of the Humane Society of New York, especially William Berloni, Janise Bogard, Sandra De Feo, Elizabeth Groves, Susan Richmond, and Anne-Marie Karash.